Country Music
HAIR

Erin Duvall

HARPER
DESIGN
An Imprint of HarperCollins Publishers

HarperCollins books may be purchased for educational, business, or sales
promotional use. For information please email the Special Markets Department
at SPsales@harpercollins.com.

Published in 2016 by
Harper Design
An Imprint of HarperCollins*Publishers*
195 Broadway
New York, NY 10007
Tel: (212) 207-7000
Fax: (855) 746-6023
harperdesign@harpercollins.com
www.hc.com

Distributed throughout the world by
HarperCollins Publishers
195 Broadway
New York, NY 10007

ISBN 978-0-06-243921-5
Library of Congress Control Number: 2015959440

Printed in China

First Printing, 2016

right: Dolly Parton

Contents

Foreword

Style and culture have always gone hand in hand, and country music has celebrated iconic style moments through the decades with the best of them. Fashion evolves, just as musical taste does, and hairstyles seem to pinpoint the trends of the season of music more than anything. I most certainly associate musical moments with the styling of the artist—whether it was the vision of Dolly Parton's sky-high platinum curls as she sashayed across the stage in a power-ballad with Porter Wagoner, or how Billy Ray Cyrus rocked America with some countrified-sass in the '90s with an "Achy Breaky Heart" and a mullet.

Hair is a creative self-expression in itself. Just as artists captivate with melody, their personal styling expresses their passion and vision to their fans. Who would Willie Nelson be without his iconic braids? Would Taylor Swift have launched into the musical stratosphere without the sweetness of her soft curls matched with the innocent teenaged-longing of "Tim McGraw"?

This journey through decades of country music and the evolution of personal expression through style and hair explores the relationship we all have with our favorite country artists, their iconic music moments, and the personal style that marked their reign over the charts.

—Cassie Kelley

left: Johnny Cash

Introduction

Country music is a lifestyle. It's rare to find a casual fan of the genre that gave us such cultural icons as Dolly Parton, Willie Nelson, and Reba McEntire. It all starts and ends with the music, but once country fans find an artist who speaks to them, who sings the words they can't find themselves, an incredible bond is formed. There's a loyalty and an allegiance created between artist and fan that allows singers to have long and lasting careers.

Songwriter and producer Harlan Howard, who cowrote "I Fall to Pieces" for Patsy Cline, famously broke down country music to its essence, stating that it is made up of "three chords and the truth." From the Carter Family to Blake Shelton, this theme can be found. The melodies are simple and easy to sing along with, and the stories strike at the soul.

In the 1920s, the Carter Family, who would later give us June Carter Cash, began performances across the nation of what we would today call country music. The songs they made famous

left: Patsy Cline

could be easily rendered at the kitchen sink or at a Saturday evening gathering by a singer of any skill level.

But prior to the '50s, the term "country music" didn't exist. Folk music is the original country music. The themes and the tales are those of the common man. Ernest Tubb is known for coining the phrase country music after he himself was referred to as a hillbilly musician. He chose the label, it is said, because that's where the majority of the people who play this type of music come from: the country. And the word seemed less derogatory than "hillbilly". In any case, country found its way into the cities—first on the airwaves of WSM AM during performances of The Grand Ole Opry, and later on the glass of Farnsworth's invention.

In the '60s, country singers were afforded an invitation into every home in America. From *Hee Haw* to *The Johnny Cash Show*, variety shows brought these iconic voices into the living rooms of those who loved their lyrics, increasing the intimacy of the fan experience. At the same time, it created increased pressure on the stars of the day: they could no longer be anonymous voices on the radio; they now had to become superstars.

With more eyes on them, country singers rose to the challenge, embracing their images. That isn't to say that style wasn't a consideration before this time. But the increased exposure that television brought amplified this need. There's a huge difference between singing in front of hundreds of people at a festival and thousands or millions on the small screen. Since the '60s, artists have evolved their hairstyles and fashion along with their music as they have grown in stature and career ambitions. Numerous icons from the genre have paved a path using their unique hairstyles and looks to advance their careers and lives.

The focus on looks, while seeming somewhat superfluous and shallow in a business that should be driven by talent, has helped build careers. This added element has drawn fans in and created another level of intimacy between them and their favorite singers. Hairstyles are emulated and lusted after. Haircuts are publicly mourned or celebrated. An artist's image is almost—almost—as important as his or her music.

There are no requirements. No one has to look a certain way. They simply have to represent themselves. Country singers come in many varieties. From mullets to mustaches or teased hair to bobs, country singers have their own distinct looks. Some wear hats and others wear wigs. Some follow the trends and others set them. Some have stylists tour with them to ensure a perfect do for every show, while others are confident with their own hair-spraying abilities.

Over the past sixty years, country singers have become movie stars like entertainment mogul Dolly Parton, helmed their own sitcoms like Reba McEntire, and created a legion of loyal lifestyle fans like Willie Nelson. They've crossed genre lines and inspired popular culture with their music and their looks—all while their fans cheered, purchased their merchandise, and followed their lead. They have built lasting relationships with the masses while perfecting their craft and influencing generations.

To this day fans still adamantly express their opinions when stars make a significant alternation to their look, the same way they respond when a sound or musical style is altered. You can't separate Dolly Parton from her over-the-top dos. Would Reba McEntire be Reba without her signature red hair? Willie Nelson will forever be the Red Headed Stranger. Hair is tied to the music and the music is tied to the hair.

THE
1960s

The Bakersfield Sound
and Bouffant Hair

The 1960s were a decade of change and tragedy. It was the era of Elvis Presley and the British Invasion. People were doing "The Twist" along with Chubby Checker and "(Sittin' on) the Dock of the Bay" with Otis Redding. Women's lib was on its way in as the idyllic families of the '50s struggled to keep hold. Society was evolving, and so was the music being created. The changes in the world directly affected a generation of listeners as well as artists.

The hairstyles of both men and women made drastic leaps over the course of the decade. Prim and proper was the way of the '50s, and wild and free would be prevalent in the '70s. Nashville was no different as it was broadcast to homes across the United States. As the music became mainstream so did the styles of those who were churning out the hits.

The country music epitome of this evolution was Willie Nelson. During the early '60s, the man who would become known as an icon the world over was residing in Nashville and making his living as a songwriter and a musician. Not only had he yet to record his classic hits, but he looked nothing like the man we know today. Nelson was clean-shaven, with his trademark red hair cut short. He was a respectable thirty-year-old, writing hit songs such as "Crazy," which Patsy Cline would record in 1961.

"I've always been aware of Willie Nelson, and I used to cover 'On the Road Again,' but it wasn't until I was twelve or thirteen that I realized that he wrote 'Crazy' for Patsy Cline," country singer Sara Evans admits. "But I really had no idea that he ever looked any different than he does now."

On November 22, 1963, the world was forever changed when President John F. Kennedy was assassinated in Dallas. The world looked on and mourned the young president's loss, which for country music fans reopened recent wounds. Months before, on March 5, they had said good-bye to their own Patsy Cline when she perished in a plane crash. Nashville wouldn't have long to recover from either loss before facing catastrophe again. In July of the following year, Jim Reeves—who topped the charts with "He'll Have to Go"—also lost his life suddenly when his plane crashed just south of Music City.

Both Patsy Cline and Jim Reeves were leaders of the Nashville Sound. By the time of their deaths, they had already launched successful careers, recording music that would long outlast them. Patsy Cline's look is frozen in time due to her tragic death. She is an iconic symbol of a time period and way of life. Her hair didn't stagnate during her career, but did stick to a simple range. Her short styles kept up with the looks popular in the late '50s and early '60s, which would have been a necessity for a woman on the road.

The '60s was a time before modern hairdryers. Primping for those with long hair was much more tedious than it is today, especially when you were living on a tour bus. According to Nashville hairdresser Earl Cox, his former client Barbara Mandrell, who played steel guitar for Patsy's touring band, learned a backup trade while on the road with the songstress (luckily, her own entertainment career took off).

"Barbara was very young, in her early teens," says Earl, owner of Trumps Salon in Nashville. "Patsy would have Barbara do her hair for her on the road. It was a tedious process and took hours."

Celebrity makeup artist and hairstylist Neil Robison offers an explanation of how Patsy, and Barbara, would achieve the songstress's looks.

"Generally, you'd do that with a roller," he explains. "You roll one row of rollers one way and then the next row another way. One goes down, one goes up. Then it has to be mapped out to where the part is going to be, if it's going to be in front of the ear or behind the ear. Cool, then completely brush it out."

He warns that waiting for the rollers to cool is essential for this look.

"I don't know that Patsy Cline had naturally curly hair, but I would say she probably did," he adds. "Naturally curly hair when brushed out is going to look finger-waved like Patsy's."

Before her death, Patsy became friends with an up-and-coming country starlet. Loretta Lynn, who would go on to be one of the biggest stars in country music, started out humbly with her first single, "I'm a Honky Tonk Girl." The song and her look reflected Loretta's simple upbringing in Kentucky. She kept her hair long and manageable. At times she would add volume to the top, but never reaching the monumental heights of her contemporaries in the '80s.

However, as fame found Loretta, she found it difficult to keep her hair in any decent condition. Tammy Wynette's stylist, Nanette England, remembers the aftereffects of overzealous fans.

"She was so funny," Nanette recalls. "She'd come in and her hair would be all messed up from being cut on by fans. Chunks of it would be gone. Fans would cut her hair for souvenirs while she was signing autographs."

Over the years, Loretta's hair has remained nearly the same: long, brown, and natural. This look and her personal stories of struggle have helped her walk a fine line of superstardom and normalcy. In the '70s and '80s, Loretta would become known for her princess look. She would wear large, extravagant ball gowns in public, but she remained the "Coal Miner's Daughter." She is loved among the country music community for both her meager upbringing and her decadent showmanship.

Alongside Patsy Cline and Loretta Lynn was Dottie West. Together, the three inspired a generation of artists and fans. West began to make her presence on the country scene known in the '60s. "Here Comes My Baby" took her to the top ten on the country charts and opened the door for her first Grammy for Best Female Country Vocal Performance.

In country music, the burgeoning fashion icon of the '60s was a young girl from Sevierville, Tennessee. By the mid-'60s, Dolly Parton had finished high school and moved to Nashville, where she began building her career and name. Before the end of the decade she was already a full-fledged style icon, sporting an array of hairstyles on *The Porter Wagoner Show*.

She became known during this time for various versions of the bouffant—a precursor to the big hair of the '80s. Dolly's style and hair were on point in every single appearance. Granted, it didn't hurt that she was also in her late teens and early twenties as she began her career. While she consistently wore the bouffant, she occasionally took the height of her hair a step further to create the coveted beehive. This was a time-consuming look to achieve, as hairdresser Earl Cox explains.

"A bouffant is long on top, and most ladies would have it cut to the nape of their neck and then slightly angled around the face," says Earl. "You need length on top to make a bouffant work. You would roll it up with rubber rollers, then tease the devil out of it, then smooth over all the teasing with a finishing comb."

Dolly wasn't the only one sporting the bouffant, though. Jackie Kennedy made headlines as the only First Lady at that point ever to have worn the do. Back in Nashville, it was also seen on Kitty Wells, who became known as the Queen of Country Music after breaking down gender barriers in the genre in the '50s. Kitty became the first female solo artist to top the country charts when she recorded the response song "It Wasn't God Who Made Honky Tonk Angels," which called out Hank Thompson's tune about losing his love to the night life, "The Wild Side of Life."

Perhaps the male equivalent for the time was the pompadour. Not nearly as tall as the bouffant or beehive, the look gave men volume and bounce at the top of their heads. Elvis Presley and Johnny Cash both famously wore the style during the '60s.

But Johnny Cash's look wasn't as rebellious as he was at that time. He was arrested several times during the '60s, adding legitimacy to his insurgent songs. The Man in Black had a difficult time fitting in over the years. Some claimed he was a rock act, while others insist he was a classic country singer. In 1965, he was banned from the Grand Ole Opry after breaking the stage lights at the Ryman Auditorium with a microphone stand. Although the Outlaw Movement didn't come about for a few more years, the building blocks were there as early as the '60s.

"In 1964 or '65, I lived in the Riviera apartments," stylist Nanette England recalls. "Johnny Cash rented an apartment over there, and he had nothing but a tuxedo. He'd wear tuxedo pants rolled up, and a tuxedo shirt tied up. All he had were stage clothes. He didn't have any blue jeans."

That obviously didn't matter to his friends, though. "He and Willie Nelson and Waylon Jennings would all come over and sit and pick in Johnny's apartment," she adds. "I was nineteen years old, and I'd go over and smoke pot with them and have the best time. There was never any light in there. It was always real dark because they were all stoned. I'd be sitting there like a dumbass nineteen-year-old, thinking, 'Well, this is fun.'"

Nanette adds that she never became a fan of marijuana, citing that it made her paranoid, and quickly found her way back to vodka.

In 1968, Cash married June Carter, who can single-handedly be credited with turning his life around. The pair lived a storied romance that has been admired in songs—venturing all the way into the pop world with Katy Perry's "The One That Got Away"— and films such as the 2005 biopic *Walk the Line*, starring Joaquin Phoenix as the troubled singer and Reese Witherspoon as his love.

By this time, June was a member of the Carter Family band, which her mother, Maybelle, had cofounded in the '20s, but now consisted of Maybelle and her three daughters. As the members of the band changed, so did their looks, moving away from the shelling look of the '30s to popular styles of the '60s. Country star Ty Herndon is convinced he knows how June and her sisters Anita and Helen achieved their looks.

"My momma had the same hair," he says. "I know this for a fact, they had two or three hairpieces, and they were on Styrofoam heads in the bedroom. I'm saying this because I recognize that hair because of my mother. I was raised in south Alabama on bluegrass and country music. It was common for me to see three hairpieces in rollers on a Styrofoam head in my mom's bedroom. She would go to sleep with a scarf on her head. She'd get up, fix the hairpieces, and bobby-pin them to her hair, making it like a foot tall. My mother had to be in her twenties—she had me at nineteen—so she was in her late twenties, wearing those awesome, cool hairstyles. And I know the Carter Family had to have had foam heads."

Merle Haggard has had a long career and storied life. Today he's often thought of solely in connection with the Outlaw Movement of the '70s, a mistake that is likely a result of his bold political statements and criminal history. "Mama Tried," his legendary tune about his wild ways and his mother's attempts to reform him, could very well have contributed to this misconception as well. He even spent time behind bars for various crimes. Not to say that Merle didn't associate with founders and icons of the movement, but the Hag made his mark before the others. Before the Outlaws, there was Bakersfield.

The Bakersfield Sound is a bit of a misleading term as well. While it was and still is associated with the city in central California, the sound of this time was developed and honed in honky-tonks across the United States. It was gritty, acoustic, and real. It was a response to the highly produced sounds that had been prevalent in Nashville during the '50s. The Nashville Sound could be compared with the pop-country sounds of the 2010s. It was polished and perfected, as were the looks. Jim Reeves and Ferlin Husky were poster boys for the subgenre, with their slicked-back hair and pencil ties.

Buck Owens, who would become the ambassador for Bakersfield, rose to fame in the late '50s and early '60s. He made quite a splash in 1963 when his song "Act Naturally"—which would later be recorded by the Beatles—became his first number one song. While his sound was less polished than the music coming out of Nashville at the time, Buck's appearance didn't stray too far from the norm. At times, his hair might have been slightly longer than clean cuts of the day, but it never reached a length that would cause controversy. Among others things, the Bakersfield Sound would go on to inspire a later generation of singers that included Dwight Yoakam and Marty Stuart.

Near the end of the '60s, Buck launched the show that would become an important part of country music history and the childhood of country music fans. *Hee Haw* was a country-themed variety show that Buck cohosted with Roy Clark for nearly twenty years. The show served as a platform for many a country singer to connect with thousands of fans at once. It also made famous the call-and-response in which Buck would say, "I'm a-pickin'," and Roy would reply, "I'm a-grinnin'."

It wasn't the only nonmusical legacy that Buck would leave, though. In 1996, the entertainer opened Buck Owens' Crystal Palace in Bakersfield. To this day, the venue, restaurant, and museum is still considered holy ground for country music. Artists take pride in playing the stage that Buck built, which is revered and esteemed in much the same way as the Grand Ole Opry stage or the Mother Church of Country Music, the Ryman Auditorium.

The Bakersfield Sound paved the way for the Outlaw Movement. One of the turning points for the sound came in 1969, when an exasperated Merle Haggard released "Okie from Muskogee." Though he was born in Oildale, California—just a few miles outside of Bakersfield—Merle was born to a pair of Okies who had moved west during the Great Depression. The singer cowrote the tune that would arguably become his signature song in response to protests against the Vietnam War. It topped the *Billboard* country chart and earned the Hag a Single of the Year honor from the Country Music Association in 1970.

above: Brenda Lee, *right:* Merle Haggard

above: Patsy Cline, *right:* Willie Nelson

left: Loretta Lynn, *above:* Dolly Parton

above: Tammy Wynette, *right:* Kitty Wells

The Carter Family

Johnny Cash

left: Buck Owens, *above:* Dottie West

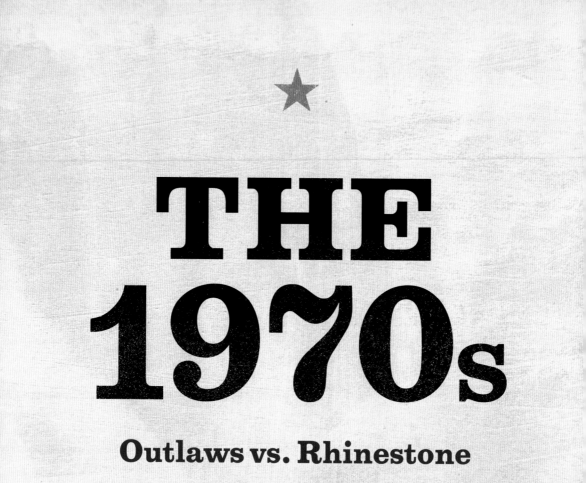

THE 1970s

Outlaws vs. Rhinestone Cowboys

In terms of sounds and style, the 1970s took everything from the '60s and built upon it. Stereotypes were exaggerated. Alliances were strengthened. Just as Bakersfield was the basis for the Outlaw Movement, the Nashville Sound opened the door for the Rhinestone Cowboys. It was during the '70s that the split in the genre became most apparent.

Country music has always been about the fans, about the people that the singers represent and aim to please. There are two ways to approach these people. You can either dazzle them with bright lights and big productions or you can strip it down and portray yourself as they see themselves. There's the unattainable fantasy of beauty and wealth juxtaposed with the way life is for those in rural and Middle America.

Each side had its own list of superstars. The Highwaymen wouldn't form as group until the '80s, but its four founding members—Johnny Cash, Willie Nelson, Waylon Jennings. and Kris Kristofferson—headed up the Outlaw Movement. There were female outlaws as well, like Jessi Colter and Emmylou Harris, who were both prevalent during the time.

The Rhinestone Cowboy, as Glen Campbell would come to be known, represented a cleaner look. Money was spent on Nudie suits, the popular choice of the day, and the music was more heavily produced. It sounded much more contemporary than what the Outlaws played, fitting in with the popular music of the day, but the topics were still genuinely country.

"Wichita Lineman" is about a workingman who needs a vacation and needs to get home to his love. Glen took the song to the top of the country charts in 1968. The following year he went number one with "Galveston," a tune about a solider dreaming of home and the sweetheart he left there. Both topics relate to country's core demographic: hardworking Americans.

By the '70s, Glen had appeared in several films, even starring alongside John Wayne in the original *True Grit*. He wasn't spending his days in the dirt or on the range. His rodeo was under the spotlight, playing on his own variety show, *The Glen Campbell Goodtime Hour*, or signing autographs as he walked down Broadway in a suit. He had become the "Rhinestone Cowboy," which—although he didn't write it—became his signature song after its release in 1975.

Also setting the standard for glamour during this time was Tammy Wynette. Over the years, she'd come to be known as the First Lady of Country Music. Her life was filled with love, loss, and controversy. She approached it all with poise and style. Her former hairstylist, Nanette England, remembers the night she first met Tammy. It was moments before the annual CMA Awards were to take place at Nashville's Ryman Auditorium, and Tammy was in no shape to be seen by her fans.

"That night [her husband] George Jones pulled up in the back alley behind the Ryman. He was as drunk as a bicycle and it was pouring down rain, and he put Tammy out and she came in looking like a drowned rat," recalls Nanette, whose sister Jan was also a hairdresser. "Jan saw her come in and said, 'Come over here.' Roy Acuff had his own private dressing room. There was one room that everyone else went to and then Roy had his own special room. She took Tammy in there and did her hair so nobody saw her looking like that."

That act of kindness prompted Tammy to continue her relationship with Jan. "She fell in love with Jan and asked my sister to go on the road with her, and then they got pregnant at the same time," explains Nanette, referring to Tammy's pregnancy with her daughter Georgette. "When Jan got pregnant, Tammy needed a hairdresser and along came Nanette. I went on the road and we did a lot of shows like *The Johnny Cash Show*."

Tammy may have employed hairdressers, but she kept a firm grip on her style. "Tammy was a hairdresser," Nanette explains. "She kept her licenses current, always. She knew exactly what was going on. Tammy Wynette was no dummy about anything that was going on except men. She was pretty stupid about her men. She had her license current, I'm sure, the day she died. She knew makeup, she knew the way she wanted to look. She was tough."

Before Tammy moved to Nashville and married George Jones, she had already had three children with her first husband. Her strength showed in the way she handled her family, Nanette explains.

"She came here with three babies and she used to put [her daughter] Tina's little dress under the leg of a bed," she says. "She didn't have running water, so she'd have to go down to the well to get it. She'd put Tina's dress under leg of the bed so she couldn't go anywhere. That's how she figured out how to do it."

According to Nanette, it's that attitude that made working with Tammy such a joy. The singer wasn't prone to emergencies or melodrama. The work came first. "One time, we stopped on the side of the road and went in and I washed her hair in the sink in a bathroom of a truck stop," she recalls. "You made the best of a bad situation."

One situation in particular could've ruined an entire European visit, if Nanette hadn't been quick to find a solution.

"We were in London and I needed to touch up her roots, and they had broken my bottle of developer and I had no developer with me," she remembers. "I got somebody at the hotel to take me to a supply house, and I didn't know anything about their products, so I bought what I thought would work and put it on her and it broke all of her hair off."

Luckily, some fast thinking and a long-distance call saved the day. "It was about a quarter of an inch long," Nanette continues. "I called this friend of mine who was a chemist for Lamar Laboratories and he said, 'Castor oil stops breakage.' Castor oil with a cream conditioner, about ten drops to an ounce, and it stops breakage immediately. I did that and got her hair back. I have one client and she doesn't have any hair! That wouldn't have been a good thing."

In 1975, Tammy ended her volatile marriage with George Jones. George's alcoholism and physical abuse during this time has been well documented. While they were married, the pair recorded a string of albums together, and they would reunite years later for two more projects.

Tammy went on to have several more relationships in the public eye, including one with a Hollywood hunk who is also known for his hair—facial hair, that is.

"She dated Burt Reynolds," Nanette recalls. "We went on his set when he was making *Semi-Tough* in Florida. He was great. He was so funny. She had a house in Jupiter, Florida, then—that's where he had his ranch. He'd come over and have dinner and we'd tell funny stories. He was very personable and fun."

Despite her own relationship ups and downs, Tammy Wynette is forever known for "Stand by Your Man," a song she cowrote with her producer, Billy Sherrill, and took to the top of the country charts in 1968. It was a complete flip from the song she released immediately before, "D-I-V-O-R-C-E," that told the tale of the aftermath of a failed marriage. "Stand by Your Man," as the title suggests, laments the difficulties of being in a relationship, but professes the importance of working through those difficulties and staying with the relationship at hand.

Songwriter George Richey and Tammy Wynette were married in 1978, on a day Nanette associates with the beginning of the end for the country music darling.

"What he did was hide it," says Nanette, referring to the physical pain Wynette endured following a hysterectomy. "I heard him say, 'As long as I'm living, you'll never want for any pain medication.' They had their wedding date set for July 6 and I gave her my notice on July 3. I said, 'I love you, I'll be here for you, but if you marry him, it's a done deal.' If you look back at what happened, all the Tennessee Gentlemen [her band] quit. He ran everybody off who cared about Tammy."

When Wynette died suddenly in 1998, there were many allegations made by her daughters regarding Richey's part in their mother's demise. Her body was exhumed and further tests were performed, but Richey was never charged in his wife's death. Richey died in 2010.

Another glamour icon who came into her own during this time was Dolly Parton. Though she'd been a presence in the '60s, as had Tammy, both rose in status during the '70s. The two women took great pride in their appearance and approached their looks with the same method.

"It was wigs," announces Nanette. "I'd have about ten or fifteen wigs, I'd fix them all. We'd go on the road and then I would put a wig on her head. That was it. How hard was my job? It was just easy. Tammy was so easy. She always had a wig on. It was never her hair. Never."

Wigs give versatility and time to an artist who is always on the go. Being on tour comes with numerous time constraints. There's travel time from venue to venue, and then there are sound checks that have to be performed with each new stage to ensure an artist sounds her best and can hear herself. There are also scheduled meet and greets, time that an artist needs to take in order to visit with local radio stations and media or even her fans. This doesn't even take into account that artists are people who have lives back at home that require attention. Wigs give an artist extra time to handle all of the other responsibilities before them.

"They were synthetic wigs, so they stayed great," Nanette explains. "Her real hair was baby fine. Not good hair. It wouldn't have held up through a show. I'd touch her hair up, because she bleached it. Not all the time, but on the weekends or if we were going somewhere. The front of it, maybe we'd comb out over the wig, but usually not."

Wig upkeep wasn't something she ever worried about. "You wash it in Spic and Span or whatever you want to, and then you shake it out and it curls back up. You comb it out and it does its own thing. You can't put heat on a synthetic wig, though."

And when times got tough, the wigs came first. "The bus caught fire in Waco, Texas, once, and I was like, 'OK, get under that bus and get the wigs and the costumes out,'" she recalls. "I was directing traffic."

Dolly Parton became known for big, larger-than-life wigs and styles during this time period. She also became known for her impeccable and eye-catching makeup, something a young Sunny Sweeney caught on to early.

"Dolly Parton's makeup was the tops," the country singer says. "I wanted to look like her with the bright red lipstick and the thick eyeliner. I'm from East Texas, so that kind of comes naturally anyway. We're brought up that way with blue eye shadow in seventh grade."

In 1970, Dolly earned her first number one song with "Joshua." She followed it up with several more, including "Jolene" in 1973 and, in 1974, "I Will Always Love You," which would later become associated with Whitney Houston after her performance of the tune on *The Bodyguard* soundtrack. Dolly also served as a cast member of *The Porter Wagoner Show* through the early '70s, regularly performing duets with the show's namesake.

The era of variety shows on the small screen was the birth of fashion icons in country music. That isn't to say that fans hadn't tried to emulate the looks of stars prior to this point, but for the first time country singers were actively and continually plotting the course of popular fashion.

"Tammy and the bigger stars set a trend," Nanette says. "There wasn't a thought about New York and L.A. looks. The country music girls would've never worn a Barbra Streisand bob. We were in our own world here in Country Music, USA. We were setting the stage for it. We didn't need to look elsewhere."

Another artist who wasn't taking cues from anyone else was Linda Ronstadt. In her early twenties, Linda was a fresh face with a vibrant attitude. She fit the vibe of the '70s. She had a natural, girlish look that appealed to both men and women. Her hair had bounce and life to it, but never came close to the heights worn by the glam squad in their stage performances. From short curls to long layers, Linda stood out. It was a look that a young girl like singer Deana Carter admired in the '70s.

"I have always fought for a more natural look," Deana says. "On the red carpet, you see people have updos or unique braids or styles and all that. I will always default to the Farrah Fawcett look. I still to this day try to find people who can cut layers properly. It's not just from the earlobe down, I want layers in the crown so that it can look natural and have body. I think that's a timeless, all-American girl look."

Linda has been called the First Lady of Rock and the Queen of Rock, but her beginnings were closely aligned with country music. Linda walked the line between rock and country in much the same way as the Eagles did. Their music is undoubtedly rock and roll, but its sentiments and sounds can also appeal to the traditional country listener.

Linda even saw herself on the country chart from time to time, topping it in 1975 with "When Will I Be Loved." This crossover success brought the young singer to Nashville. On one particular trip in 1969 the young maven shared the stage with a country legend, performing on *The Johnny Cash Show*.

"Linda Ronstadt was on the show with Johnny and they were going to sing a song together," Nanette England remembers. "They had a big platform out in front of the stage with La-Z-Boys for Johnny and his wife, June. Well, June was sitting out there and she said, 'That girl doesn't have any panties on. She can't sing with my John like that.' So they went over to Cain-Sloan's and got Linda some panties."

Linda may have gone along with the wardrobe change, but according to Nanette, that doesn't mean she liked it. "She's coming back in and Johnny passes her and says, 'Linda, you got your drawers on?' and she says, 'Yeah, but I sing better bare-assed.'"

During the '70s, Johnny Cash was maturing as an artist. The '60s had included arrests and success. He'd had hits with "In the Jailhouse Now," "Folsom Prison Blues," and "A Boy Named Sue," but it was in the following decade that he became a full-fledged Outlaw—in title only, of course. In addition to hosting his own show, he enriched the world of music with a multitude of tunes that would become classics, such as the Kris Kristofferson–penned "Sunday Morning Coming Down," his own composition "Man in Black," and "One Piece at a Time," a song in which the narrator steals car parts from his employer over a long period of time in order to build a comical, yet free, vehicle.

The '70s were a time of growth for Cash, who was settling into life with his new bride. Nanette, who spent time behind-the-scenes of *The Johnny Cash Show* with Tammy Wynette, has a strong opinion of the pair's relationship.

"June pretty much controlled Johnny," Nanette says. "He was funny. She was ate up with herself. She didn't want 'my John,' as she called him, around any of the women on the show. He was fun and cute to be around. He was spontaneous."

For the first time, Johnny's hair started to move away from the short, kept look he had worn in the '50s and '60s. The change seems more drastic on him, a former serviceman, than any of his Outlaw counterparts. His hair never reached the lengths of Willie Nelson or even Waylon Jennings, but began to take on a life of its own. His locks began to reflect Johnny Cash's own attitude of independence.

The Man in Black wasn't the only one to opt for this physical transformation. By the '70s, Willie Nelson was well on his way to becoming the man we know today. He had been a presence in country music in both the '50s and '60s, making his own records in addition to serving as a songwriter. As a performer, though, he didn't make a significant impact on the country scene until the '70s.

He'd begun to transition from a clean-cut, flattop look and embrace the freedom of the decade. He let his naturally ginger hair grown long and began keeping a full beard. It wasn't a unique look for the time, but something about the way Willie wore it was different, so much so that his hair fueled one of the most iconic albums of his career.

In 1975, Willie Nelson released *Red Headed Stranger*, which garnered him his first number one single with a song that became one of the most beloved in country music, "Blue Eyes Crying in the Rain." The album and the song became the solid foundation on which the singer-songwriter made his membership to the Outlaw Movement.

Willie Nelson found his way into the hearts of country music fans with a rich but unassuming voice and a folksiness that appealed to the genre. A native Texan, Willie Nelson's songs have leaned toward the western side of country and western, telling tales of love and loss and life with the land.

Also finding his footing in country music at the time was frequent Willie Nelson collaborator and future member of the Highwaymen Waylon Jennings. Like Cash and the Red Headed Stranger, Waylon started out in the '50s as sharply dressed as the rest. His early gigs included a stint in Buddy Holly's band, and he nearly died in the same fateful plane crash on "the day the music died" in 1959. But he gave up his seat to J. P. Richardson, otherwise known as the Big Bopper, and opted to ride the bus to the band's next tour stop. It was a decision that haunted Waylon for years.

After a string of releases in the '60s, Waylon found hits in the '70s with "Good Hearted Woman," "I'm a Ramblin' Man," "Luckenbach, Texas," and "Are You Sure Hank Done It This Way." The albums released during this time built a legacy that made Waylon and Willie among the most admired men in country music. In 1999, Clint Black would even cover "Are You Sure Hank Done It This Way," changing the title and the words to "Are You Sure Waylon Done It This Way." And as Sunny Sweeney will admit, Waylon still has a reputation as a sex symbol.

"A dude's hair needs to be messy," Sunny says. "Sometimes I look at Waylon and I'm like, 'He's so hot.' If I would've been an adult when he was a megastar, I would've been on him like white on rice. I would've been chasing after that guy. Any of those guys that wore the leather and looked dirty all of the time. I think dirty-looking men are hot [*laughs*]."

Jessi Colter, who was not only one of the leading females associated with the Outlaw Movement at the time but also Waylon's wife, would agree with Sunny's sentiments, and she has.

"I was born too late," Sunny explains. "I've told Jessi that before: 'I needed to be there.' She said, 'Waylon would've been on you girl. He would've been chasing you.' That's coming from his wife, so I guess that's OK [*laughs*]."

The last of the Highwaymen, Kris Kristofferson, moved to Nashville in 1965 with hopes of achieving his musical dreams. Despite personal pressures, the singer-songwriter would do just that. In 1973, he topped the charts with "Why Me," but Kristofferson is mostly remembered for his significant songwriting contributions.

He wrote "Sunday Morning Coming Down" for Johnny Cash and "Me and Bobby McGee" for Janis Joplin, to name two. Additionally, while it was never a single, his own recording of "Help Me Make It Through the Night" has also become a fan and artist favorite.

Kristofferson would continue to write and record for years to come. As previously mentioned, he would also join up with fellow outlaws Willie Nelson, Waylon Jennings, and Johnny Cash to form the Highwaymen in the '80s. Like his cohorts, Kristofferson's appearance was unkempt. He was always in need of a shave—that is, if he wasn't wearing a full beard—with hair long enough to be considered long.

With his life rooted in country music, Kristofferson was also able to make a go of it in Hollywood, starring in films such as

Convoy, *A Star Is Born*, and the aforementioned *Semi-Tough* with Burt Reynolds.

The now-iconic Emmylou Harris began making waves in the '70s. She would grow to become one of the most beloved songwriters in country music history. Her music was always on the fringes, incorporating rock styles and sounds as she associated with acts like Gram Parsons and the Band, but country music has claimed this living legend.

"Being a little girl in the '70s, it was all about how long can your hair be? How straight can it be?" Deana Carter remembers.

"I remember loving Emmylou Harris's hair," Sunny Sweeney adds. "It was long and straight and parted down the middle. There was one record cover where she was on a front porch and her hair was just straight. I wanted to be her."

Emmylou's look was universal, rather than being tied to the Nashville looks that Tammy Wynette and Dolly Parton were culti-vating. Her look and her music crossed genre lines.

"To me, back then it seemed like people were more connected stylistically across the board," Deana explains. "It wasn't like, 'Oh, this is rock and roll and this was country.' Everyone was dressing the same way."

During the '70s, Emmylou earned numerous country hits. "Together Again" and "Sweet Dreams" would take the peak position on the country charts in 1976. "Save the Last Dance for Me" and "Blue Kentucky Girl" would both break the top ten in 1979, leading up to another number one in 1980 with "Beneath Still Waters."

The '70s were also the start of Crystal Gayle's career. She was the younger sister of Loretta Lynn by nineteen years, and her hairstyle was similar to Emmylou's. She wore it long and straight, a look that has only changed in length over the past forty years. Gayle is known for more than just her sleek dark hair, though. She topped the country charts with "Don't It Make My Brown Eyes Blue" in 1977 and even found success on the adult contemporary charts. The song is credited with making the album *We Must Believe in Magic* a commercial success, and Gayle became the first female country artist ever to earn a platinum album (an honor given for selling more than one million units).

Lynn Anderson also saw her share of crossover success in the '70s. She had spent the late '60s as a regular performer on *The Lawrence Welk Show* before leaving to focus solely on her country career. In 1970 she released "(I Never Promised You a) Rose Garden," which would become the biggest song of her career. The single topped the country charts and made it to number three on the pop charts, in addition to breaking the top ten on several international lists.

right: Tammy Wynette

above: Crystal Gayle, *right:* Kris Kristofferson

above: Emmylou Harris, *right:* Waylon Jennings

left: Willie Nelson, *above:* Lynn Anderson

above: John Prine, *right:* Janie Fricke

Dolly Parton

Barbara Mandrell

THE 1980s

The Bigger the Hair
the Closer to God

Everything was bigger in the 1980s. It was the Texas of decades. There's likely a hole in the ozone that was created solely by the hair spray of the ladies of country music during this time period. The country girls—like many women in the '80s—wanted locks that loomed over their heads. As the saying goes, "The bigger the hair, the closer to God."

"Bigger was better," songstress Deana Carter recalls. "To this day, I don't like my hair to look flat. It's something about the features in my face, being Southern, whatever it is. I like more body in my hair. I've heard Reba [McEntire] and Wynonna [Judd] and all those people joke about 'the higher the hair, the closer to Jesus you are' and all that stuff, but I like it full but not sprayed too much. It needs to have some body."

Sunny Sweeney agrees, remembering, "My hair in my seventh-grade school picture was so big that it went outside the frame. I remember combing it out and flakes of hair spray would come out."

Obviously, the natural traits of a girl's hair determined how much time and money was need to "jack it to Jesus," if you will.

For instance, Deana Carter has naturally curly/wavy hair. "It's not super frizzy," she explains, "so I was able to use a curling iron to get it big. That said, if you had straight or curly hair, you got a perm in the '80s."

That was the secret to the big hair. Not hair spray and not teasing combs. The trick was the perm.

"It was the early '80s, so everybody had to have a perm," celebrity stylist Earl Cox explains. "That was just the look: perms and big, big hair. If you have the perm, it swells that hair and it will allow you to do anything. At that point in time, short hair was not a thing."

Now you know why perms became so relevant during this time. "That's why girls did the perms," he continues. "They would diffuse it and then let it dry naturally. Then they'd go in and tease it and make it big. The perm did all the work for you. If you got a bad perm, you were screwed."

To this day, the debate still rages on over who had the defining big hair of the '80s. One of the front-runners, though, was a redheaded girl from Oklahoma who would become a superstar.

"I had the big eighties hair," country singer Sara Evans admits. "I didn't have the money to really look like any of them, but I tried for sure. Reba was my biggest obsession. She was the one who touched me the deepest with her music. I was always fascinated by her voice and her song choice: how sad some of her songs were."

By the '80s, Reba was starting to gain traction on country radio, slowly but surely breaking her way into the top twenty on the country charts. In 1982, she earned her first chart topper with "Can't Even Get the Blues," and many important people have contributed that career-defining moment to her hair (or at least they should). The future media mogul had a leg up on her comrades. Her hair was made for the volume.

"She has really curly hair; a lot of people don't realize that," explains her current stylist, Neil Robison. "It's spiral curly. I always say if she looks at water, her hair curls."

Sandi Spika was Reba's hairstylist during the big hair days, and Neil walks us through how she achieved the songstress's signature look: "Sandy would hot roll Reba's hair, which is already kinky curly. Then she would take one roller out, tease it, spray it, and then take another curler out, and so on. That's why her hair was so big."

No matter the length—short or long—the volume of one's hair was key to many people's images in the '80s, but this was especially true for Reba.

Another contender for the big hair title was a superstar we've mentioned before. "Dolly Parton had the best big hair in the '80s," declares Sunny Sweeney.

The '80s were the decade that showed the rest of the world the greatness that is Dolly Parton. Her film career started to blossom during the decade and earn her fans who hadn't previously been exposed to her music. In 1980, Dolly made her film debut in *9 to 5*, alongside Lily Tomlin and Jane Fonda, as one of three fed-up working girls ready to take drastic measures to earn respect. In 1982, she starred opposite Burt Reynolds in *The Best Little Whorehouse in Texas*, as the most admired madam around, and by the end of the decade she became everyone's favorite and most quotable stylist in Louisiana as Truvy in *Steel Magnolias*.

Still opting for wigs, rather than teasing her own hair, Dolly wasn't one to miss the trend. She stuck with her token blond color and wore wigs that gave her hair as big as any other girl's in country music.

Patty Loveless made a name for herself in the '80s—another fiery redhead, but this one hailed from Kentucky. She embraced the big hair of the decade and began touring with the stars of the day, including Reba McEntire. Her hair easily welcomed height, but rather than taking it long, she held steady at a mid-length that landed around her shoulders.

The big hair movement went hand in hand with the dirty hair movement. Stylists and beauty queens the world over have claimed that dirty hair is easier to style. Neil Robison says that's not necessarily true.

"Everybody is different," he explains. "Half my clients are better with dirty hair, and the other half need to wash every day. I have clients with curly hair that, if you put heat on it and then they go out in the humidity, that hair goes all flat. Then I have curly-haired clients who have the opposite happen."

Patty Loveless would have gotten to see this firsthand. She came to Nashville for the first time in her teens and was lucky enough to find herself backstage at the Grand Ole Opry. She would later tell stories to her hairdresser, Earl Cox, about watching all her idols have their hair done prior to the show, an experience that stuck with her through adulthood.

Over the next twenty years, Patty would earn some of country music's top honors. She was inducted into the Grand Ole Opry in 1988 and earned both the Academy of Country Music and the Country Music Association's Female Vocalist of the Year titles. Her traditional country voice would also take her to the top of the country charts five times.

In the 2000s, Patty would embrace traditional country music and bluegrass more so than in her early career. In 2001, she released a pure bluegrass album, *Mountain Soul*, which was greeted with critical acclaim. A decade later, she appeared on Miranda Lambert's *Four the Record*, singing backup on the song "Dear Diamond."

Barbara Mandrell was a superstar in '80s. So much so that she was able to host and act on the *Barbara Mandrell and the Mandrell Sisters* variety show in the '80s. The show included everything from comedy sketches to musical performances and made the singer's appearance more important than ever.

"I vividly remember that Barbara Mandrell had this long curly hair," stylist Earl Cox recalls. "The first time I ever met her, we had like a three-hour consolation about what to do with her hair; she wanted to be updated."

Unlike the singers' stationed in Music City, Barbara had other ideas. "I personally feel like Barbara brought her style, fashion, hair, and she made country music become more mainstream by the TV show she had," he explains. "If you look back, the hair was always very current. The show was filmed in L.A., so she used some L.A. people then. She had the longer, permed hair, and I cut her hair off. I cut it into a bob, and that was a big deal. In those days, that was a big stretch. We did the bangs and the bob. It was on the CMA show, and she came out and I had done her hair smooth and short, and you could hear the gasp in the audience when she walked out."

Janie Fricke is another songstress who rose to fame in the '80s wearing the hairstyles of the day. She began her career as a backup singer for the likes of Conway Twitty, Dolly Parton, and

Lynn Anderson. By the '80s, she'd found her style, vocally and fashion-wise. She became known for ballads such as "Down to My Last Broken Heart" and "I'll Need Someone to Hold Me (When I Cry)," and took home the Country Music Association's Female Vocalist of the Year title in 1982 and 1983.

The ladies of country music weren't the only ones with big hair in '80s. Conway Twitty, who stylist Ty Herndon says had the best hair in country music, wasn't afraid of the hair spray. Over the years, the crooner had it all. He started out in the '50s with a flattop that morphed into a pompadour, but before we knew it Conway's hair was big and bold. Another one with slight curl to his hair, volume was no problem for Conway. Through the '70s he wore his hair slicked back, but let it grow longer than during his early years.

By the '80s, he'd let the hair grow long on top and the sides, letting the curls make the distinct look for which he became known. Over the course of his career, Conway earned fifty-five number one songs, leaving country music such iconic songs as "Hello Darlin'" and "Louisiana Woman, Mississippi Man," a duet with Loretta Lynn. He held the record for the most chart-topping singles until George Strait surpassed it in 2008. He began the '80s at the top of the charts with "I'd Love to Lay You Down," earning a total of twelve number ones before the decade was out.

"My Heroes Have Always Been Cowboys," "On the Road Again," and "Always on My Mind" were among Willie's first few chart toppers of the '80s. The decade gave birth to the Willie Nelson whom we know today—the one with long red braids and a graying beard. When the stories are told and the book is closed, that is the Willie Nelson who will be remembered.

"At concerts, they sell the Willie Nelson headband and bandana with the braids that you put on," says Sunny Sweeney. "I remember having one of those when we were younger, and my sisters and I would put it on. I didn't ever know he'd been clean-cut until I started getting into music."

On the other end of the spectrum was Ronnie Milsap. His look, while long, was conservative compared to Willie Nelson's and lacked the volume of Conway Twitty's top. Unlike most country music, Ronnie Milsap's is piano driven. A nonconformist look for a nonconformist sound. Nanette England remembers being on the road with the blind singer, who always knew when Tammy Wynette approached.

"Ronnie Milsap would always say, 'Oh, Tammy, it's so good to see you,'" Nanette recalls. "He always knew who you were. He got it from the perfume. He knew who all of us were from our perfume. He'd call us by name."

Tammy Wynette was living a new life in the '80s. She'd married George Richey and cut ties with many old friends, including her longtime stylist Nanette England. She began working with legendary manager Stan Moress, who took the opportunity to address the songstress's image.

"I had several meetings with her and her husband, George, and we decided to take drastic action restyling hair and make-up and wardrobe," Stan remembers. "This took about three or four months to get together. We made a commitment to each other that we were going to follow through. I got this wonderful hairdresser from L.A. who was willing to go to Florida to cut her hair. Everything was set up, and she called me the morning of the day he was flying, and he had already left, and Tammy was in tears. She was sobbing. I said, 'What's wrong?' She said, 'I don't know if I can do this.' I said, 'It's too late; he's already on the plane. It's a lot of money that we're talking about and a lot of his time.' I did it nicely. We were on the phone for about twenty minutes. I said, 'Just meet him and don't say no. Just hear what he has to say.'

"I wanted until he landed and got to Tammy's house, and four hours later she called and said, 'I'm madly in love with this guy. He's cut my hair off, he's colored it, and you're going to love it.' When I saw the photos I was astonished. I thought he'd do a good job, but he did a great job. I can't remember the guy's name."

This may seem overdramatic for the everyday person, but an artist's image is as important as their music.

"It's like taking the same show out on the road for five years; people want to see something different," Stan explains. "She had a lot of hidden beauty, and when you put the right makeup and the right hair and the right clothing on her, she was a whole new Tammy. People were loving it. It changed her career. She wanted to work more and work better venues. People were excited about her again, and it was one of the greatest experiences that I've had in the music business."

"Her image was everything to her," adds Earl Cox, who worked with Tammy later in her life. "A few days before she passed away, I was at her house coloring her hair. She was in hard-core pain, but it meant so much to her to make sure that her hair was going to look right. Some people may think that's crazy, but for Tammy it was everything. There's an image, and it's old school."

The Cowboy Hat

One of the best heads of hair that you never get to see is George Strait's. The Texan was blessed with lush, flowing brown hair, but as a genuine cowboy he hides his locks under a Stetson. This is a rarity in country music.

"I went all through the '80s hanging out in a cowboy hat," Ty Herndon explains. "When I got signed to Sony in 1994, that's the first thing they said: 'We've got to lose the hat because you have hair.' I noticed Blake [Shelton] lost his hat too. I still pull my hat out from time to time during my shows. I've always had a great barber, a great stylist. Over time, I've probably spent thousands and thousands on product."

Perhaps it's a ploy to save on hair products, but since his debut in the '80s, King George has kept his hair under wraps. While others were playing with length and styles over the course of the decade, George opted for his traditional style. His music has always been a throwback to the early days of country music, tending toward two-steps and waltzes rather than the trends of the moment. Whether it's hair or music, George Strait is a traditionalist.

Popular culture enthusiasts seem to be under the impression that cowboy hats have been prevalent throughout the history of the genre, but if you look back over these pages, you'll see a lack of Western wear. The notion that country singers wore cowboy garb was ingrained on the social consciousness by the singing cowboys of the early days of TV and film. Gene Autry and Roy Rogers wore cowboy hats and Western fringe as they sang their songs of working on the range. But the cowboy hat didn't really take hold in country music until the '80s.

Like George Strait, Garth Brooks came onto the scene in the '80s. Much like his hero, Chris LeDoux, Brooks wore the cowboy hat. So much so that it is rare to find any photos of the showman without it. Unless, that is, his Southern manners come out and he removes it out of honor or respect, as he has done at a few awards shows. It is said that one of the reasons Garth Brooks never became an international superstar was because of the cowboy hat. Apparently, European audiences had a difficult time accepting that dominant piece of his image.

Then there are artists who fought long and hard to avoid the hat. Travis Tritt, who rose to fame the same year as Garth Brooks, made a point to avoid the trope.

"That was one of the things that I rebelled against from the very beginning," he says. "Not that I had anything against cowboy hats—a huge part of my audience wore cowboy hats. That was a big part of who followed me and listened to my music, but at the time that I came out with my first single, which was the same year that Alan Jackson, Clint Black, and Garth Brooks all came out with their first singles, they were very clean-cut, they wore starch-pressed shirts and cowboy hats. I did not. Not that I had anything against it. It was just one more way of showing that I was different. It was one more thing that set me apart from the rest of the group. That was discussed at the very beginning when I first came to Warner Bros.: 'You could even go with a hat.' I said, 'I'm not a hat act. That's not me. I never wore a hat on a regular basis when I was playing in the clubs. I think to try and change the image into something I'm not comfortable with is a mistake.' I fought against that and was able to resist the urge to put on a cowboy hat like everybody else."

There are also gentlemen who, as Ty Herndon alluded to earlier, need the help of a hat. Kenny Chesney, whose hair thinned quite a bit over the course of his career, is almost never seen without some sort of cover, whether that be a cowboy hat or a baseball cap.

Alan Jackson, though, seems to be another like his compadre George Strait, who isn't lacking in the hair department. In fact, Alan kept a long mullet under his cowboy hat for years, much to the dismay of his stylist Melissa Schleicher, who often nudged him to lop off his locks. Short or long, Alan's golden mane has remained under his trusty cowboy hat for more than twenty-five years.

above: Dottie West, *right:* Reba McEntire

The Judds

June Carter Cash and Johnny Cash

above: Keith Whitley, *right:* Tammy Wynette

above: Willie Nelson, *right:* Linda Ronstadt

THE 1990s

Mullets and Meltdowns

The title says it all. Country music in the 1990s was all about mullets and meltdowns. Almost all the men in the genre—minus King George, of course—sported the trendy mullet, most famously Billy Ray Cyrus. And in terms of meltdowns, the bonds between country singers and fans were tested when some of the genre's most beloved women (and men) cut their locks.

"Burn" is a radio term for the point when a song has been played so much that listeners will change the station when they hear it. In Top 40 radio, it's common for songs to burn. But it's said that the last song country radio burned was Billy Ray Cyrus's "Achy Breaky Heart" in 1992.

The song defined an era of the mullet. It, and Billy Ray, are forever connected to the look that has been described as business in the front and party in the back. Nearly every man in country music during this time had some form of mullet, but Billy Ray has unwittingly become its ambassador for rednecks everywhere.

"He's been so gracious about the mullet," Deana Carter says. "He represented a whole generation of how people wore their hair. Even in the rock world, you had Bowie with a mullet."

Cyrus held on to the look until the late '90s, when he finally decided to cut his hair. However, for the father of Miley Cyrus, cutting his hair didn't mean transitioning to a flattop or a crew cut. Cutting his hair meant cutting it to his shoulders.

However, rumor has it that the day Cyrus chose to make this transition, Miley, who couldn't have been more than five, became hysterical. Tears flowed as the locks were cut. The future star of *Hannah Montana* wasn't the only person upset by the cut. Fans sent letters to Cyrus detailing their disappointment and dissatisfaction with his new do.

"Grooming and hair have always been important," Ty Herndon explains. "I had the early Blake Shelton. Actually, Blake Shelton had the early Ty Herndon. I was there a little before him."

Ty shares the shares the secret of how to style the mullet: "I always used a hairdryer and slicked it back and put the hat on. I never really had the short on the sides; it was just pulled over my ear. It was slicked back and long, which was fantastic."

Over the years, Blake Shelton has also become synonymous with the mullet. Although he didn't come on to the scene until the late '90s, releasing his first single, "Austin," in 2001, he did wear the style much longer than his predecessors.

"Blake Shelton had the mullet of all mullets," remembers Deana Carter. "He had the whole business in the front and party in the back."

The fact that Blake wore the hairstyle longer than others paired with the fact that he had such curly hair definitely gives a fighting chance for the mullet crown. The mullets of Tim McGraw, Kenny Chesney, and even Garth Brooks can't compare to Blake Shelton's. When they're asked about it these days, modern country singers have a hard time figuring out what exactly the appeal of the mullet was.

"I think it was the ability to ponytail it and look professional," Deana Carter says. "You had a choice maybe? You can wear it to work and be respectable but then you don't lose your total wild side. 'I'm grown up. OK, I'm not grown up.' And it was the evolution of the hippie movement. You could ponytail and go to church and then take it out and be on your boat drinking beer in the afternoon. It's the same as with sleeveless shirts."

Speaking of the "hippie movement" in the '90s, Willie Nelson didn't have the mullet, but his hair had reached epic lengths. He continued to let it grow and to keep it braided during appearances and performances. His reputation for marijuana use was also becoming more prevalent. In 1994, he was arrested for possession, a charge that wasn't his first and wouldn't be his last.

Lucky for Willie, not having a mullet means he can avoid Sara Evans's wrath.

"I hate the mullet. I always hated it," Sara admits. "I always thought of it as trashy and redneck. I was never attracted to it. There is only a certain type of guy who can have long hair and make it look good. To start with, he has to have great hair that will grow long and not be frizzy and curly. There aren't a lot of men who can pull that off. I never thought it was a good idea."

Garth Brooks, who entered the scene in what is referred to as the class of '89, found megastardom in the '90s. He began his career with a modest mullet. Garth's hair never had the volume or thickness of Blake's. Instead it was fine and straight and took sanctuary under his hat.

As he and his fellow "classmates"—Alan Jackson, Clint Black, and Travis Tritt—each began to grow in popularity, they took distinct paths with their manes. Each new male had seen their first bit of success in 1989, but each would make their mark in the '90s in a different musical way.

Garth would become one of the bestselling artists of all time—putting him in categories with the Beatles and Elvis Presley—and would define himself with his high-energy stage performances. As the years progressed, his popularity soared, and so did Garth, who as he found new ways to entertain crowds went so far as to fly over them.

Travis Tritt took another approach. Over the course of the '90s, the Georgia native became known for pairing his songs with cinematic music videos. Tritt had nearly fifteen top-ten hit songs during the decade, making him one of its defining voices. His hair evolved with his persona.

"Before I ever got signed to a record deal, I was playing biker bars, holes-in-the-wall, some really rough places, just trying to get a name out there, trying to get an opportunity to showcase my music wherever I could," Travis Tritt explains. "Obviously, after coming out of that background, when I got signed to my first record deal, in 1987, I was simply a product of the places I had been playing for so long. I had real long hair. I had hair down to my chest. The whole, I guess you would call it, Southern rock, Outlaw, biker look."

That look didn't last long, though, once he signed with Warner Bros. Records. "When I got signed to the record label, that was one of the things that we butted heads over from the very beginning," he explains. "They wanted me to cut my hair, simply to try and make me more palatable to radio stations. The way it was described to me was, 'What if we've got a radio programmer who's got a seventeen-year-old son who grows his hair out long like yours and he's been trying to get him to cut it and he says, 'But, Dad, you're playing Travis Tritt's music. He's got hair as long as mine or longer.' That's not going to go over well. They convinced me to cut my hair, and as soon as I did, I regretted it. I felt like I had sold out. I made my mind up that I would let my hair grow back out as the career grew. I grew my hair out longer then than it was when I first got to Warner Bros., because the career went ballistic and was on fire."

Tritt put so much energy into his hair because he considered it to be a valuable part of his persona. "I always felt comfortable with the long hair in those days because it was one more thing that gave me an identifying factor to my audience," he says. "I knew my audience listened to the same things I did: they liked country music, they liked rock music, they liked Southern rock, they liked the blues, they liked a lot of different things. Having that look was one more thing that made them identify with me and my music and me as a personality."

His hair eventually ventured into mullet territory but stood out from his comrades thanks to his ability to style the short bits much like bangs.

"There are some people who called it a mullet, but I don't ever think of myself as having a mullet," Tritt explains. "When I think of a mullet, the first thing that comes to mind is Billy Ray Cyrus. He had business in the front, party in the back. I had long hair.

It was a littler shorter in the front, but never to the extent that cuts like Billy Ray's were. People call the hairstyle I have today a mullet, so I don't know."

The problem with long hair, as many men have learned, is keeping it manageable onstage. Especially when you're onstage on a hot summer day with the sun beating down on you. "I have a tendency to perspire a lot, and with long hair it's just that much more," Tritt admits. "I know in the very early days when I was playing an outdoor gig in the middle of the summertime, I might take it and put it in a ponytail just to keep it manageable and cooler. I always thought that was part of the attraction, because I grew up in the '70s, when you had these pictures of everyone in entertainment—Lynyrd Skynyrd, the Allman Brothers, Peter Frampton—everybody had long hair, and you see them onstage and they're soaked in sweat and the hair isn't perfect by any stretch of the imagination. It's wild and all over the place. Those are some of the most iconic images, to me, of what a rock star or a music star is supposed to look like. For me, there was never any added special things I did to accommodate the hair onstage. Just go out there and let it fly."

The one constant in Tritt's look has been his mustache and beard, which remain today.

Tritt's frequent collaborator, Marty Stuart, also came onto the scene in the early '90s. Stuart had made a name for himself long before, though, as a musician. During his early career, he played with an array of bands, including the backing band for Johnny Cash. By 1989, he had signed his own record deal and begun building his own brand. He cowrote "The Whiskey Ain't Workin'" with Travis Tritt, which the pair recorded as a duet and released on Tritt's 1991 album *It's All About to Change*. The two also collaborated on a tour they named "No Hats," referring to the fact that the majority of male artists at the time wore cowboy hats while they did not.

Joe Diffie is one of the definitive artists of the '90s. His distinct voice and style helped solidify what is commonly thought of as the genre's best decade. Diffie's hits covered a broad range of topics and styles, endearing him to a legion of fans.

Humor has always been an element of country music, and Diffie's voice and comedic timing provided for some of the most memorable songs in country history. "Prop Me Up Beside the Jukebox (If I Die)," from 1993, begins heavy and sincere before kicking into the lighthearted chorus. In addition, "Pickup Man," which topped the charts in 1994, is a love song about a man and the vehicle that has always helped him to meet members of the opposite sex.

Then there are his love songs. With its simple and relatable message, 1993's "John Deere Green," a story about a small-town love, will continue to be a fan favorite for generations to come. And who wouldn't want a love "Bigger Than the Beatles," something the Oklahoma native depicted in his number one hit from 1995?

Diffie was able to tackle serious subjects in a serious manner. His debut single "Home," which went to number one in 1990, is a nostalgic look at the narrator's origins and how they shaped the man he became. He even toasted dreams that don't come true in his 1992 top-five hit "Ships That Don't Come In."

Diffie's work as a songwriter and artist have made him a significant figure in the history of country music. In 2013, Jason Aldean paid tribute to the tunesmith in the song "1994," name-checking not only Diffie but his tunes as well.

The '90s were much more dramatic for the women, who had to endure massive meltdowns in regard to their styles. The first big controversy came in 1993, when Reba McEntire took the stage to perform at the annual CMA Awards ceremony. The controversy had nothing to do with her gorgeous red locks, but instead the stunning red dress she had chosen to wear.

When the superstar took the stage, her mesh top became see-through under the intense stage lights and appeared more risqué than intended. The mesh, which actually came up to Reba's neck and then moved into long sleeves, seemingly disappeared, leaving the singer with a plunging neckline.

Reba isn't the only singer to make the mistake of not testing a performance outfit in stage lighting. In the '70s, Tammy Wynette experienced a similar wardrobe malfunction, but was able to catch it in time.

"She had a dress one time that when she got up on the stage during a rehearsal, you could see through it," stylist Nanette England remembers. "So I pinned pillow cases around her so you couldn't see through. [Designer] Nudie [Cohn] made the dress. It was this great white dress that came down and had a panel down the front. It was beautiful. She didn't have a slip with her, so I pinned one pillowcase in front and one pillowcase in back."

Perhaps the biggest shock of the '90s came when Faith Hill released her music video for "You Can't Lose Me." She had been on a roll since 1993, when her debut single "Wild One" topped the chart right out of the gate. She quickly became a fan favorite and followed up with "Piece of My Heart," which she also took to number one.

Fans fell in love with her small-town charm and long blond locks. She wore her hair big, not as big as her '80s counterparts, but there was volume—until 1996, that is. "You Can't Lose Me" is a touching song about the relationship between mothers and daughters, and the video featured Faith on the beach with a new, short do.

"My father loves Faith Hill," Sunny Sweeney remembers. "He thinks she is the most beautiful person on the planet, and I remember he was really upset when she cut her hair. To me, as a woman, it's very liberating. I've never cut it that short, but I've cut eight or nine inches and been like, 'Oh my God, I don't have hair anymore, it's great. It takes me two minutes to fix my hair.' Then I always hate it and grow it back out. I remember my dad was devastated by it. I feel like it's part of your job to evolve your look and change, just like you do with your music."

"I remember when Faith cut her hair," Sara Evans says. "That was a huge deal. People were so mean about it. I couldn't believe it. I felt so bad for her. She is so beautiful, she could do anything and look great, but typically people do not like her to have short hair."

What's interesting in retrospect is that Faith wasn't trying to make a statement with her hair. Stylist Earl Cox was the person whose scissors made the cut heard 'round the world, and he explains the reason they made the choice.

"Faith Hill had the long curly hair—hers is naturally curly— and we cut her hair off," he says. "The backstory to that is that her hair was longish, and she'd gone somewhere and had her hair braided. Because she was really blond, and they'd braided it so tight, when they took the braids out her hair was breaking and splitting and tearing. She said, 'Earl, we got to cut it.' And it became her signature look for quite some time. Faith has always been very progressive in her hair looks. She does it before anyone else does it."

She wasn't the first or last artist to face the problem of breaking hair. In a day and age when dyeing and blow-drying are commonplace, singers have to take great care to keep their hair healthy. Sunny Sweeney recalls a time when she was in a similar situation.

"In April or May of 2012, my hair was falling out because of my bleach," she remembers. "I had gone really blond, and I was blow-drying it all the time and curling it. The same girl has done my hair for ten to fifteen years in Austin. She was like, 'We're going to dye your hair brown.' And I said, 'No, we're not.' She goes, 'Yeah, we are, because your hair is falling out.' Or you can cut it off. I was so uncomfortable, because it's not me. I actually ended up getting a song out of it, because this woman insulted me, but she was trying to give me a compliment. People feel that because you're in public that they can tell you what they think."

The song Sunny refers to is "Backhanded Compliment," which describes an incident in which someone tells her they prefer her as a blonde.

"I feel like you need to watch what you tell people, because if you work at a desk and only know six people, it's a little bit different than when [someone famous] gets a bad haircut or goes out on a limb and pictures are taken of you that you can't veto," Sunny explains. "There are angles that you can't veto. It's hard being put under a spotlight, but it's always what you signed up for."

Martina McBride was another big star of the '90s who decided to cut her hair, and coincidentally, she also went to Earl Cox.

"I cut all her hair off," Earl admits. "She wanted to make a statement. Martina came on the scene and had this look that was brown hair, and everybody had long hair. Martina made a conscious decision to cut her hair, and I think it made people take notice. She wanted to be current. She wanted to have a new look and a new vibe. Short hair is not for everyone, but those two in particular can really wear it well."

The most important thing about both Faith and Martina's cuts was that they were able to wear them well.

"They're two beautiful girls and they have a great way of carrying things off and they liked it," Earl explains. "If you like it, then you're going to carry it well. People ask me if I worry about styling someone's hair because it's going to be on TV and critiqued, but I don't. I think about pleasing the artist in the moment and our personal relationship."

"I remember Martina's hair when she cut her short," Sara Evans says. "I thought that was a really smart move on her part. I actually like her hair shorter."

Earl stresses, though, that there is much to take into consideration when choosing a cut, and especially when making a drastic change.

"I take in how much time they want to devote to it. The texture of their hair means everything for what type of cut you can do—their lifestyle, their body shape," he explains. "Their body shape is as important as their facial shape. It's OK to sit in front of a mirror and look at a face shape, but their body shape may not work for that hairstyle. You need to look at the person from head to toe—if they have broad shoulders, if they're tall or short. All those aspects come into play. It's more than just pulling a picture out of a magazine and saying, 'I want this.' I don't believe in doing a style that isn't going to be relatively easy to maintain, because I have some clients who will spend any amount of time to get their hair how they want it to look. I'm here to help guide you, and you know what you're comfortable with. I've got tons of clients who would look great in short hair, but they don't feel comfortable in it. I'm very careful about suggesting things too far away from what they feel comfortable with."

Martina McBride is known for singing songs of female empowerment. Her hair reflected the strength she was singing about. As the years went on, Earl remembers taking her mane even shorter as she became more comfortable.

"It was a short, short pixie cut, really textured and really different. Very boyish," he says. "I think for her we had gradually gotten shorter and shorter. Part of it was that she was on the road, she has very thick hair, and she was playing outdoor concerts and things like that. She will tell you she only knows one way to do her hair. The shorter we went, the easier it was for her being on the road. It was a combination of seeing photos of cuts that she liked and what would work for her hair texture out on the road. She's always been progressive in that aspect. It's how she wanted to express herself. She's a strong woman, and short haircuts portray strength. She looked like what she was singing about. She likes strong looks."

Another essential piece of finding looks that work best on a certain person is trust. The relationship between the stylist and the individual is essential. When an artist knows that the person they're working with has their best interests in mind, they become willing to take chances and explore options.

"There was one thing we did with Martina when she did a video in New York called 'Wild Angels' and her hair was already on the shorter side," Earl explains. "I remember doing a situation where we had curled it, and I had literally taken the curlers out and left the curls in, as opposed to brushing them out. That was very new. I remember one of the people with the record label said, 'Martina, I don't think this look is going to appeal to people in the Midwest. I don't think they're going to understand it. I think we should do something else.' Martina was so awesome. She looked at me and said, 'Earl, do you like it?' And I said, 'I personally think it's very cool. The setting is perfect.' She told the person, 'I like it, Earl likes it, so we're going to leave it.' She made a conscious decision to do something out of the box and not be tied down to anything. I applaud her for going with it. 'We're going to do this and see how this works.'"

The safety net that is provided when working with length is wigs, and in the '90s, hair extensions began to show their abilities as well.

"Late '80s, early '90s was when I started working with extensions," Earl explains. "The call was to add length and volume. For the longest time, we didn't do them in Nashville. A lot of times we'd use them because they wanted to let their hair grow out."

Aside from artists like Dolly Parton, wigs began to fall out of fashion in the '90s. But an exception was made for music video shoots.

"Doing music videos, you use many wigs," Earl says. "I love working with wigs. Back in the day, you didn't have a lot of options for wigs. There were synthetic wigs, and you had to try and make them look good. Wigs give a whole different character, and in videos that's what you are using ninety-nine percent of the time."

Music videos are usually shot with very tight time constraints. An artist's time is valuable, so most shoots take place over a day or two, with several setups. Wigs allow stylists to achieve multiple looks over a short period of time. They're also lifesavers when an artist is shooting a period piece that may require a bouffant and she's working with a pixie.

George Jones was always a timeless classic. Though he started out with a flattop, and played with some length—especially on the sides—throughout the '70s, his hair remained fairly the same with volume at the front and tidy at the ends from the '80s until his death in 2013. By the end of the '80s, his locks had begun to go white, but he was unmistakably George.

Jones spent years of his career battling with alcoholism. His struggle with the bottle is cited for ending his marriage to Tammy Wynette in 1975. The pair had produced numerous albums together prior to their divorce, which left the songstress with anxiety about not only the end of their relationship, but the end of their working life as well.

"[Band member] Harold Morrison was Tammy's comedian when I went to work for her," Nanette England reveals. "The first time we left without George Jones, we were all sitting in her kitchen, waiting to get on the bus, and she said, 'What if nobody comes? They all loved George. What if it was all about George and nobody comes to see me?' We're like, 'Are you kidding me?' We're riding down the road, and we're listening to Jones's music as we go, and we sit and talk. We were riding along, and she said, 'You know, I really miss him.' And I said, 'You miss George?' And she said, 'Yeah, don't you kind of miss him?' Harold Morrison looked at me and said, 'I guess if somebody hit you in the head with a hammer every day for seven years and he quit, you'd miss that too.'"

Despite their volatile relationship, George and Tammy reunited in 1980 for *Together Again*, which included the top-five hit "Two Story House." They wouldn't work together again until 1995, when they released the album *One*.

The Judds

above: Wynonna Judd, *right:* Billy Ray Cyrus

left: Dolly Parton, *above:* Travis Tritt

Tracy Lawrence

Reba McEntire

above: Billy Dean, *right:* George Jones

left: Alan Jackson, *above:* Marty Stuart

THE 2000s

Layered and Frosted

The turn of the twentieth-first century brought highs and lows to country music. We watched some of the biggest stars of the day rise to fame and some of the most promising lights burn out. Legends found new ways to invent themselves and move along with the times. Fan favorites decided to explore other aspects of their talents, making even a trip or two to Hollywood to try their hands at the silver screen. The age-old question of what country music should sound like was on people's minds as the late '90s continued to creep in.

Many groups—as opposed to just solo artists—found their footing in the early 2000s. At the start of the decade, Rascal Flatts entered the scene with their first single, "Prayin' for Daylight," and continued with a steady stream of number one hits for the next 10 years.

The members of Rascal Flatts were at the forefront of male country artists keeping their looks stylish and put together. Of course, there have always been clean-cut and well-dressed men in country music, as we saw with the Nashville Sound movement of the '60s and the Rhinestone Cowboys of the '70s. But hair products, highlights, and frosted tips didn't become the standard in the genre for men until the 2000s. Rather than making an appointment with the barber, almost all country men were now finding a hairstylist, as their female counterparts had been doing for decades.

It was around this time that hairstylist Melissa Schleicher was finally able to convince another male client to lose his mullet. Alan Jackson was born with beautiful blond locks that he wore long under his hat for years. After what seemed like eons of asking him to lose them, Melissa won the battle, and Alan slowly, but surely, began to wear his hair to the nape of his neck.

Tim McGraw, who had been a fervent wearer of the hat, began to take off his Stetson in the 2000s. This move coincided with his choice to spend his off months in Hollywood pursuing multiple film projects such as *The Blind Side* and *Friday Night Lights*. Some have suspected that he also took some corrective measures with his hair. A main reason that a man wears the cowboy hat is to hide an imperfection. Some speculate that as the decision to lose the hat happened, Tim also invested in cosmetic surgery or hair plugs to fill some gaps.

For the first part of the decade there was no bigger band in country music than the Dixie Chicks. These three Texas women with vibrant personalities dominated the genre for a number of years. Unlike the majority of the women of the day, they were constantly updating their look for each new project. They had coordinated bleached blond hair that was styled at different lengths and in different ways. Each woman was different. Each woman was herself, a distinct part of a whole.

While legends continued their reigns into the twenty-first century, the era also welcomed a new class of stars to the table.

We saw the rise of current superstars over the course of a decade as they grew and evolved their sounds and appearances.

In 2005, Carrie Underwood became the winner of the fourth season of *American Idol* and soon released her debut album, *Some Hearts*, and its chart-topping first single, "Jesus, Take the Wheel." When fans first met Carrie she was straight off the Oklahoma farm on which she was raised. Her hair was pretty but simple. She wore it curly but free. Her rise to fame included a change that turned her into a superstar: She now wears bigger curls that are the epitome of glam. There is never one hair out of place. Carrie has grown from the girl next door into a full-fledged fashion icon.

Also gaining traction around this time was the New Zealand–born, Australian-bred Keith Urban, who had been working his way around Nashville since the '90s. Keith Urban is another victim of the famed mullet phase who has continued to keep his hair long over the years. He also continues to wear blond highlights in his hair, which offer a look of depth as they lie over his darker, natural strands. Keith has played with several different looks, but always seems to wear his hair longer than most men of his generation.

Another hot male made a big hair change in the early 2000s. Blake Shelton, the last mullet holdout, cut his hair and lost the cowboy hat. According to stylist Earl Cox, men can be more stubborn than women when it comes to their hair.

"Their image is just as important as the female's," he says. "They know what they like. Men are usually much stronger in their opinions about what they like. They're more adamant about a certain look. They won't change as much as a female artist would. If they don't wear a hat, their hair is very important to them."

left: Keith Urban, *above:* Ronnie Milsap

left: Blake Shelton, *above:* Bucky Covington

above: Brooks and Dunn, *right:* Conway Twitty

THE
2010s

Modern Men and Women

S ince the beginning of the 2010s, country music has gained favor nationwide. Country singers are national celebrities, seen weekly on the covers of tabloid magazines that were once only home to the Los Angeles and New York elite. Numerous factors have contributed to this recent welcoming by the wider popular culture.

Perhaps most significantly, Taylor Swift has become an international superstar. She grew her fan base in innovative ways as an early embracer of the power of social media. Swift and her team created a wide presence online and took advantage of every opportunity to interact with fans. From 2006 to 2009, she grew in popularity both online and on country radio. She was also approachable. She was gorgeous but not intimidating. Taylor looked like someone you'd be friends with, and you wanted to be friends with her. As she grew, and became a woman, her relationships (and thus songs) became more complex, and she began to evolve her style and look as well. She started to shun the innocent curls of her youth and opt for trendy new looks. In 2011, the superstar took a big plunge during a photo shoot for the cover of *Vogue* and got bangs. She was no longer a young girl who wrote songs about boys she lusted after and lost. She was now a woman— with bangs.

When *The Voice* debuted in 2011, Blake Shelton was a country star. Since joining the show as a coach, the Oklahoma native has become a national celebrity whose personal life is strewn across supermarket stands. As Blake became a bigger star outside of the country space, so did his then wife, Miranda Lambert. The singer-songwriter has been one of the reigning females in country music for more than a decade, but her fame has grown in the past five years due to her appearances as a mentor on *The Voice*, her Grammy wins, and her sweep of the 2015 Academy of Country Music Awards. Miranda's look has always been her own. She has a tough persona that some might align with a "bad girl" attitude. Her hair and her style have always reflected someone who wasn't going to try and look like everyone else. She's worn the short bob and the long curly layers. She's played with different tones of color. Some days she's bleached blond and others she's golden lowlights. Her career is reflective of this attitude. Since the release of her first album, Miranda has presented music her own way.

Keith Urban, Lady Antebellum, Florida Georgia Line, Carrie Underwood, Jake Owen, Little Big Town, The Band Perry, and David Nail are only a handful of the talented country singers and groups making names with their voices and marks with their hairstyles in this decade of country music.

The Future

Country music is about the fans, and no other genre has made its artists as accessible to its fans. In 1972, the Country Music Association began putting on Fan Fair, an annual festival that invited fans from all over the world to Nashville, with the goal of letting them hear and meet their favorite singers.

Stars of all levels continue to play the annual event, which is now known as the CMA Music Festival. The meet-and-greet lines are still one of the biggest draws. Artists are just as committed to this time as their fans. In 1996, Garth Brooks signed autographs for twenty-three straight hours. That kind of commitment and mutual allegiance may be responsible for the sense of ownership that fans feel toward their favorite artists.

"I think they feel a connection with us because we've always had Fan Fair, which is now Music Fest—we've always done meet and greets," Sara Evans says. "Country music comes from Middle America, small-town America. Historically, when we have gone on tour, we've gone to these small communities, to the fairs and festivals. We've always made ourselves really available to the fans. It's a shake-your-hand kind of genre, so fans feel like they know us. We feel like we know them."

Sara Evans has had her share of fan reaction, especially when it comes to her hair. In 2014, Sara decided to try a bob out and posted a photo on social media. Almost immediately there were thousands of comments, positive and negative.

"There was a huge fan reaction, and I've been growing it out since then," she recalls. "People are really, really sweet for the most part, but some people were really mad."

This can be a double-edged sword. Hair is a major part of who we are and our self-esteem. But when you're in the public spotlight, those criticisms are more abundant and seem louder than to those living quieter lives.

"I feel complimented that my fans care enough and they feel like they can tell me," Sunny Sweeney adds.

It's a wonder that looks should have such an effect on industry that is supposed to be based on talent.

"At the end of the day, it should be about the music, but the image is a big part of it," Earl Cox says.

Artists today have more access to their fans than their predecessors did. They meet them before shows, as did the stars of the '50s, but now they can also talk to them over social media. As Sara Evans demonstrated, an artist can find out instantaneously what people think about a new hairstyle or a new song. One tweet or Facebook post is all it takes.

As country music fans change and grow, so will the artists who represent them. Over the past sixty years alone, the looks and styles of country music have expanded exponentially. Country music continually embraces the fringes of the genre and grows. Tonight there will be at least one major country act playing a show somewhere with a band member who wears a Mohawk, like Brantley Gilbert's drummer Ben Sims. Even Jason Charles Miller, who sports a long goatee and a shaved head and got his start fronting the industrial rock band gODHEAD, has found a place for himself within country music.

In late 2015, the world of country music was rocked when Chris Stapleton won Male Vocalist, Album, and New Artist of the Year at the CMA Awards. Fans of the genre took to social media to express their shock that someone they considered to be unknown could make such a splash at the ceremony. This, coupled with his breathtaking performance at the show with Justin Timberlake, took Stapleton to the number one spot on the *Billboard* albums chart overnight.

"There are artists, like Chris Stapleton, who just swept the 49th Annual CMA Awards—he doesn't look or sound like anybody else that's out there," Travis Tritt says. "He's a big guy with long hair, a long beard. He doesn't look anything like any of his peers. He doesn't sound like them, either. I think being allowed to set yourself apart is something that has been needed in country music since as far back as I can remember."

Perhaps because country singers make themselves available to their audience, fans tend to stick with their favorite artists. Long after radio has quit playing an artist's music, fans remember and make a point to come out to shows or buy independently released music. They are passionate about the songs, and they buy the merchandise. They have a stake in their favorite singers' careers.

Each is making a commitment to the other. It's a symbiotic relationship: each needs the other. Country singers wouldn't be able to live their dreams if they didn't have fans accepting their music and their messages. The country fan is what makes the genre special. They drive the direction of the music with what they spend their money on and which songs they request from their local radio stations. And in even the smallest way, a singer's hair can influence those decisions.

"If you have a bad hair day, it can totally ruin your whole day," Sunny admits. "Your hair is a part of you. The way you dress is part of you. Your makeup is a part of you. All put together, it's you. I don't feel complete in an outfit until I put heels on. If my hair isn't fixed, I feel like I'm not complete; I didn't give it my best effort. You have to give your fans your best effort."

Country music will grow with its fans. We will see female country singers rocking pink or blue hair. We could see a male country singer, not just a backup player, rocking a Mohawk. If we've learned nothing else, it's that anything is possible. While some may see this as country music becoming commercial, it's truly country music embracing its influences. There's a place for country music that is inspired by the blues, techno, hip-hop, soul, grunge, pop, and the rest. As the years go on, we will see all aspects of culture represented on the streets of Music City.

right: Sara Evans

above: Kelsea Ballerini, *right:* Jake Owens

Credits

Page 3: Dolly Parton, courtesy of The Estate of David Gahr/Getty Images

Page 6: Johnny Cash, courtesy of Michael Ochs Archives/Getty Images

Page 8: Patsy Cline, courtesy of © Grand Ole Opry, LLC

Page 22: Brenda Lee, courtesy of Bentley Archive/Popperfoto/Getty Images

Page 23: Merle Haggard, courtesy of Michael Ochs Archives/Getty Images

Page 24: Pasty Cline, courtesy of Michael Ochs Archives/Getty Images

Page 25: Willie Nelson, courtesy of Michael Ochs Archives/Getty Images

Page 26: Loretta Lynn, courtesy of Michael Ochs Archives/Getty Images

Page 27: Dolly Parton, courtesy of Michael Ochs Archives/Getty Images

Page 28: Tammy Wynette, courtesy of Charlie Gillett Collection/Redferns/Getty Images

Page 29: Kitty Wells, courtesy of Michael Ochs Archives/Getty Images

Page 30: Carter Family, courtesy of GAB Archive/Redferns/Getty Images

Page 31: Johnny Cash, courtesy of Michael Ochs Archives/Getty Images

Page 32: Buck Owens, courtesy of Buck Owens Private Foundation

Page 33: Dottie West, courtesy of Michael Ochs Archives/Getty Images

Page 49: Tammy Wynette, courtesy of Michael Ochs Archives/Getty Images

Page 50: Crystal Gayle, courtesy of Michael Ochs Archives/Getty Images

Page 51: Kris Kristofferson, courtesy of Images Press/Archive Photos/Getty Images

Page 52: Emmylou Harris, courtesy of Gijsbert Hanekroot/Redferns/Getty Images

Page 53: Waylon Jennings, courtesy of Michael Ochs Archives/Getty Images

Page 54: Willie Nelson, courtesy of Tom Hill/WireImage/Getty Images

Page 55: Lynn Anderson, courtesy of Michael Ochs Archives/Getty Images

Page 56: John Prine, courtesy of Tom Hill/WireImage/Getty Images

Page 57: Jeannie C. Riley, courtesy of Michael Ochs Archives/Getty Images

Page 58: Dolly Parton, courtesy of Harry Langdon/Getty Images

Page 59: Barbara Mandrell, courtesy of Michael Ochs Archives/Getty Images

Page 72: Dottie West, courtesy of Harry Langdon/Hulton Archive/Getty Images

Page 73: Reba McEntire, courtesy of Steve Eichner/WireImage/Getty Images

Page 74: The Judds, courtesy of Michael Ochs Archives/Getty Images

Page 75: June Carter Cash and Johnny Cash, courtesy of Chris Walter/WireImage/
Getty Images

Page 76: Keith Whitley, courtesy of Jim Shea Photo

Page 77: Tammy Wynette, courtesy of Harry Langdon/Archive Photos/Getty Images

Page 78: Willie Nelson, courtesy of Beth Gwinn

Page 79: Linda Ronstadt, courtesy of Jim Britt/Michael Ochs Archives/Getty Images

Page 95: The Judds, courtesy of George Rose/Hulton Archive/Getty Images

Page 96: tWynonna Judd, courtesy of Jim Smeal/Ron Galella Collection/Getty Images

Page 97: Billy Ray Cyrus, courtesy of Ebet Roberts/Redferns/Getty Images

Page 98: Dolly Parton, courtesy of Sam Emerson/Polaris

Page 99: Travis Tritt, courtesy of Michael Ochs Archives/Getty Images

Page 100: Tracy Lawrence, courtesy of Beth Gwinn/Getty Images

Page 101: Reba McEntire, courtesy of Tim Mosenfelder/Hulton Archive/Getty Images

Page 102: Billy Dean, courtesy of Ron Galella/Getty Images

Page 103: George Jones, courtesy of Jim Shea Photo

Page 104: Alan Jackson, courtesy of Paul Natkin/WireImage/Getty Images

Page 105 and back cover: Marty Stuart, courtesy of Randee St. Nicholas

Page 110: Keith Urban, courtesy of Paul Natkin/WireImage/Getty Images

Page 111: Ronnie Milsap, courtesy of Allyson Reeves-Land

Page 112: Blake Shelton, courtesy of Paul Natkin/WireImage/Getty Images

Page 113: Bucky Covington, courtesy of Calli Hume Photography

Page 114: Brooks & Dunn, courtesy of Ronald C. Modra/Sports Imagery/Hulton
Archive/Getty Images

Page 115: Conway Twitty, courtesy of Jim Shea Photo

Page 123: Sara Evans, courtesy of © 2014 Robert Ascroft

Page 124: Kelsea Ballerini, courtesy of Photographer Jeremy Ryan, hairstylist Chrissy
Marie (I Can Make You Blush)

Page 125: Jake Owens, courtesy of David McClister

Front cover: Barbara Mandrell, courtesy of Michael Ochs Archives/Getty Images

Thank you to...

Lauren Jo Black for making the introduction that made this book possible.

Rebecca Hunt for a great idea and taking a chance.

Everyone who took me seriously when I said that I wanted to talk about hair, especially Earl Cox, Nanette England, Sunny Sweeney, Neil Robison, Sara Evans, Kelsea Ballerini, Deana Carter, Ty Herndon, Joe Don Rooney, Susan Nadler, Beville Dunkerley, Denise Carberry, Dawn Delvo, Jules Wortman, Jensen Sussman, and Olivia Hanceri.

Al Schiltz, Mike Martinovich, and Stan Moress for always answering when I call.

Bev Moser, Beth Gwinn, Jim Shea, and the Grand Ole Opry for a stunning batch of photos.

Colleen Kelley Horn, Katie Butcher, Lauren Cowling, Kelly Sutton, Liz Lee Schullo, Bill Crutchfield, Ashley Hertzog Embry, and Jackie Monaghan for your enthusiasm and support.

Dave and Angie Duvall for, ya know, my life.